# THIS IS A COMPUTER.

# IT IS BUILT FROM HARDWARE.

THE **HARDWARE** NEEDS **INTRUCTIONS** TO WORK PROPERLY.

# THESE  INSTRUCTIONS

ON / OFF

IF / THEN

END

LAUNCH

# ARE CALLED SOFTWARE .

ON / OFF

IF / THEN

END

LAUNCH

# SOFTWARE IS THE PART OF THE COMPUTER

# THAT YOU **INTERACT** WITH.

To: grandma@home.com
From: alittledreamer@home.com

Hi grandma,
    How are you? I can't wait
to see you next week!

# IN ORDER TO CREATE SOFTWARE,

# CODE IS A LANGUAGE

```
Server
1
2 Sub Food Test ()
3
4 If Range ("FoodInput")="Vegetables" Then
5    Range ("Result")="Yes"
6 Else
7    If Range ("FoodInput")="Fruits" Then
8        Range ("Result")="Yes"
9    Else
10       If Range ("FoodInput")="Candy" Then
11       Range ("Result")="No"
12  End If
13 End If
14
15 End Sub
16
```

# THAT THE COMPUTER CAN UNDERSTAND.

```
Server
1
2 Sub Food Test ()
3
4 If Range ("FoodInput")="Vegetables" Then
5    Range ("Result")="Yes"
6 Else
7    If Range ("FoodInput")="Fruits" Then
8        Range ("Result")="Yes"
9    Else
10       If Range ("FoodInput")="Candy" Then
11       Range ("Result")="No"
12   End If
13 End If
14
15 End Sub
16
```

OH, YOU'RE RIGHT!

# CODE TELLS THE COMPUTER'S HARDWARE

```
Server
1
2 Sub Food Test ()
3
4 If Range ("FoodInput")="Vegetables" Then
5    Range ("Result")="Yes"
6 Else
7   If Range ("FoodInput")="Fruits" Then
8       Range ("Result")="Yes"
9   Else
10     If Range ("FoodInput")="Candy" Then
11     Range ("Result")="No"
12  End If
13 End If
14
15 End Sub
16
```

# WHAT TO DO AND WHEN TO DO IT.

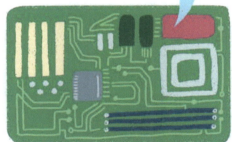

# SOFTWARE ENGINEERS WRITE CODE

# TO MAKE PROGRAMS.

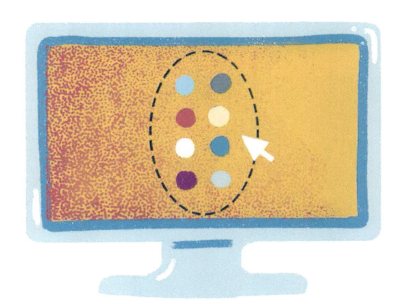

# A **PROGRAM** IS MADE UP OF LOTS OF **CODE**.

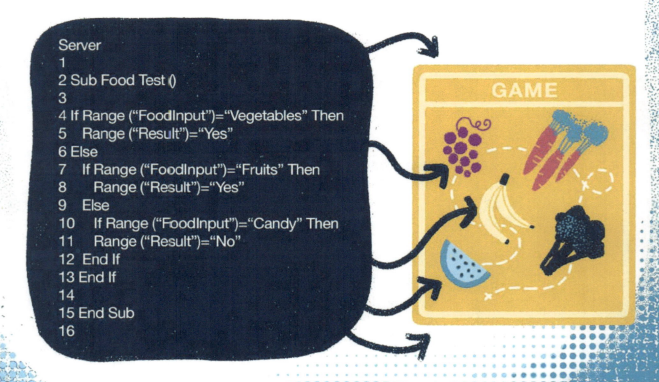

```
Server
1
2 Sub Food Test ()
3
4 If Range ("FoodInput")="Vegetables" Then
5    Range ("Result")="Yes"
6 Else
7    If Range ("FoodInput")="Fruits" Then
8       Range ("Result")="Yes"
9    Else
10      If Range ("FoodInput")="Candy" Then
11      Range ("Result")="No"
12   End If
13 End If
14
15 End Sub
16
```

GAME

# PROGRAMS INCLUDE APPS, GAMES

# AND INTERNET BROWSERS.

# WHEN YOU WRITE A PAPER,

# SOFTWARE TELLS THE COMPUTER HOW THE WORDS SHOULD APPEAR.

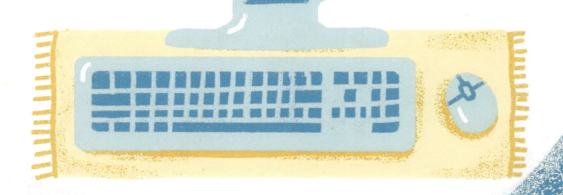

My Summer Vacation

I am excited to go on vacation.
We will have a lot of fun playing
outside and swimming in the pool.

# WHEN YOU SEARCH FOR A WEBSITE,

# SOFTWARE TELLS THE COMPUTER WHERE TO GO.

www.summerfunsearch.com

1. Fun places
2. Vacation for kids
3. My summer trip
4. Sunscreen for outside

# SOFTWARE IS IMPORTANT

# FOR MANY DIFFERENT ACTIVITIES.

# IT'S A GREAT **BIG** WORLD, WITH LOTS OF OPPORTUNITIES...

# WHEN YOU **GROW UP**, YOU CAN BE A SOFTWARE ENGINEER!